The Yakuza: The History of the Notoriou

By Charles River Editors

ヤクザ

The word Yakuza written in katakana

About Charles River Editors

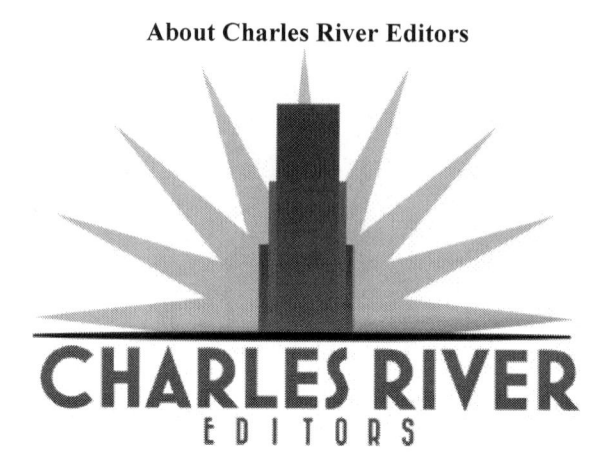

Charles River Editors is a boutique digital publishing company, specializing in bringing history back to life with educational and engaging books on a wide range of topics. Keep up to date with our new and free offerings with this 5 second sign up on our weekly mailing list, and visit Our Kindle Author Page to see other recently published Kindle titles.

We make these books for you and always want to know our readers' opinions, so we encourage you to leave reviews and look forward to publishing new and exciting titles each week.

Introduction

An 1870s picture of full body Irezumi tattoos commonly found among Yakuza members

The Yakuza

"Strong leaders understand that action cures indecision." – Toyotomi Hideyoshi, 16th century samurai

A pack of men in sharp, tailored suits and dark sunglasses strut down the street. Their eyes are shielded, but the icy scowl on their faces is a clear sign to stay out of their paths. A few of their collars hang open, showing off a glimpse of the vibrant and intricate ink work on their chests, and presumably, their entire bodies. Tattoos are the norm these days, but then one suddenly spots a man with a peculiarly pint-sized pinkie. Perhaps it is only a deformity, but upon a closer look, it appears that the entire upper half has been sliced cleanly off, almost as if it were done intentionally.

Since the beginning of civilization, crime and injustice has existed. At the same time, gangs in all shapes and sizes have been around, from rebels, dissidents, and rogue soldiers to the average circle of miscreants loitering in alleys and behind convenience stores. In Japan, a gang of a different breed would arise – one underscored by honor, respect, family, and a code of ethics. They are the Yakuza.

The Yakuza claim to be the Robin Hoods of the Far East. While they may lean towards the other side of the law, justice is all they truly aim for. After all, for a time, these tattoo-covered "thugs" have even been praised by the public. On the other hand, most are quick to say otherwise. Either way, the Yakuza is a nefarious network of stone-faced, theatrically tattooed families, with descendants that continue to make even the most seasoned of authorities quake in their shoes.

Are the Yakuza honorable rebels, or are they simply just another army of power-hungry punks? *The Yakuza: The History of the Notorious Japanese Crime Organization* explores the organization's origins, and some of the most powerful families under the Yakuza name. It also takes a look at the inner-workings of the hierarchical organization, their infamous tattoos, and the conflicting acts of terror and charity carried out by one of the most fascinating and controversial crime syndicates in the world. Along with pictures and a bibliography, you will learn about the Yakuza like never before.

The Yakuza: The History of the Notorious Japanese Crime Organization
About Charles River Editors
Introduction
    Genesis
    The Way of the Yakuza
    Year of the Yakuza
    Icons and Adversaries
    Crashing Tides and Public Discontent
    Angels and Demons
    The Modern Yakuza
    Online Resources
    Bibliography
Free Books by Charles River Editors
Discounted Books by Charles River Editors

Genesis

"Luck exists in the leftovers." – Ancient Japanese Proverb

Ravishing geishas in flowing kimonos with intricate black buns and pretty flowers in their hair, their faces painted porcelain-white. Breathtaking scenes of nature rendered beautifully in woodblock print, and aged parchments showcasing columns of calligraphy in faded black ink. Extravagant tea ceremonies, captivating *kabuki* performances, and suspenseful court music played by bamboo flutes and pear-shaped string instruments. This is only the tip of Japan's rich and colorful culture.

Every year, people from all around the globe flock to Japan for the *hanami*, or flower-viewing festivals, to peruse the stunning rows of cherry blossom trees in various shades of pink and white. Some visit Japan just for a taste of authentic sushi and other fresh seafood, as well as their mouthwatering selections of fried tempura and noodles of all girths swimming in flavorful broth. Japan is famed for its handsome skyscrapers and traditional architecture, bizarre but compelling variety shows, and their unrivaled innovations in technology and gaming. The magnetic nation continues to earn a spot in the top 10 of the most visited tourist destinations every year.

Much less advertised is the seedy underbelly of Japan, governed by one of the most powerful and influential organized crime syndicates in the world.

One of the most widely recognized hallmarks of Japanese culture is the samurai. The first samurais arose in feudal Japan during the Heian period, which began in the early 8th century. The first generation served as armed bodyguards of sorts for the obscenely wealthy landowners that had strayed from the Fujiwara clan, the family of ruling regents at the time.

The word "samurai" means "those who serve," summing up their purpose as warriors for hire. In Japan, samurais are often referred to as "*bushi*," a product of the term "*bushido*," or in English, "the way of the warrior." The *bushido* is a strict code of honor and conduct devised by the samurais. The *bushido* code consisted of 8 virtues, and was highly influenced by Zen Buddhism. The first was "justice," the most highly regarded of all virtues. Justice, which stems from righteousness, provided a samurai with the ability to make the right decision, by using reason, rather than emotion. The second virtue was "courage." Courage was not dictated by one's ferocity and initiative for aggression, but was needed for virtuous decision-making. The third virtue was "mercy." If one possessed the ability to kill, they, in turn, would have to display an equal amount of benevolence and understanding to those in need.

Discipline was a crucial part of a samurai's character. The fourth virtue was "politeness," which reminded samurais to exhibit courtesy, good manners, and proper respect to elders at all times. The fifth virtue was "honesty," which taught a samurai to choose character over riches. The sixth was "honor," and the seventh, "loyalty" to their superiors and brothers. Finally, there was the virtue of "self-control." Samurais were to adhere to the highest of all moral standards, as the samurais prided themselves on honor and integrity.

By the mid-12th century, Japan had entered the dawn of its feudal age. The emperor's power over the public began to wane. Affluent landowners and military leaders had taken control of all Japanese territories, and the emperor became nothing but a mouthpiece. This military dictatorship, the first of its kind in Japan, was called the "shogunate," headed by shoguns. The shogun's second-in-command was known as a *"daimyo."* Samurais served as mercenaries and minions to the *daimyo,* vowing to support, uphold, and achieve all commands by any means.

As the samurai culture developed, so did the significance of their swords. Aspiring samurais were taught to live by their sword, as it was a symbol of their honor. A separate art of sword-making evolved, which saw advancements in sword-molding techniques, and handles fashioned in numerous designs, including different leathers, sharkskin, and gold and silver trims. The most common weapon of choice was the *katana*, which were long, narrow, and curved swords. Samurais also battled with short but efficient *tanto* knives and *tessens,* which were iron fans often used to signal troops.

Though samurai attire experienced subtle changes over the years, their distinctive body armors and thigh guards are generally composed of oblong steel plates joined together with leather or sticky, gum-like substances. They wore helmets called *"kabutos,"* which featured a central dome made with similar plates, a steel neck guard, a chin cord, and a unique crest perched on top of it.

A 19th century picture of a samurai

By the 16th century, the beginning of the Edo period in Japan, the various samurai families across the nation had turned on each other. It was a samurai-turned-politician, Toyotomi Hideyoshi, who persuaded the warring families to let go of their grudges and live in harmony alongside each other. From then on, the samurai classes began to dwindle. The samurais still existed, many continuing to sport full armors inside their kimonos, but they became spiritual and moral leaders. Until the 19th century, villagers sought out the dying breed of warriors for wisdom and guidance.

A contemporary depiction of Toyotomi Hideyoshi

It was said that these samurais had a certain aura about them. Oftentimes, they resorted to brutality and violence to carry out their tasks, but they were concurrently praised for their loyalty to the *bushido*. They walked about the villages with a confident strut and unbreakable composure, leaving the locals both shaken and mesmerized. Samurais were far from the scum of society. Perhaps the only thing they had in common was how easy it was to spot one in a crowd.

In the Jomon period, which lasted roughly from prehistory to 300 BCE, the flourishing cities of Osaka and Edo (now Tokyo) attracted hordes of new settlers. As expected, crime swelled. To combat the growing crime rates, the *irezumi* was introduced. This term, which means "to insert ink," is one of the earliest known cases of tattooing. While many view tattoos as artistic expressions on the body, back in the day this was used as a form of branding punishment. Prostitutes, gamblers, thieves, murderers, and other criminals were marked with different symbols on their arms and foreheads. Some prefectures dotted or crossed the foreheads of their wrongdoers. In others, the number of lines inked onto the culprit indicated the number of times they had committed a crime. This was practiced in Hiroshima, but instead of horizontal lines, they formed an embarrassing Japanese character – veteran criminals forever carried the word "dog" on their foreheads. Perhaps this is why the stigma associated with tattoos is one so prevalent in Japanese culture and still exists today. In 2016, over half of public pools, bath homes, and *onsen* (hot springs) owned by Japanese hotels and resorts prohibited tattooed guests.

The early 17th century saw Japan transition into the Edo period. Often characterized as the end of the Japanese Dark Ages, it was certainly one of the most pivotal points in Japanese history. With the help of Hideyoshi and the powerful *daimyo* Oda Nobunaga, the first Edo shogun, Tokugawa Ieyasu, merged Japan into a "centralized feudal" government that would reign for 2 centuries.

A contemporary depiction of Tokugawa Ieyasu

A contemporary depiction of Oda Nobunaga

The centralized feudal system operated under a hierarchical power structure. Equal portions of lands and authority were allotted to 300 *daimyo*. The enforcement of the *"sankin kōtai"* system, which had been developed during the age of warring states, ensured that all *daimyo* were now of equal rank and status. They were owners to nearly identical bank accounts. All were ordered to serve in court by rounds, as well as pay hefty taxes to aid the funding of public and construction projects for the community.

The development and advancement of culture and technology propelled Japan into the modern age. Castle towns were home to exuberant villages teeming with business barons, creative spirits, and impressive *yamashiros*. These were "mountain castles" and fortresses, admired for their slanted tile roofs with multiple tiers, and remarkable zen gardens. Castle towns soon became one of the most dynamic destinations for manufacture and trade. Money rained down upon a budding class of merchants and artisans.

Daimyo were expected to alternate between living and guarding their own, as well as the Tokugawa castle. They were never to question the shogun's orders, and inconvenience, regardless of magnitude, was never a factor. Many found themselves laden with immense pressure, as they were required to maintain the same standards between the Tokugawa and their own estates. This constant maintenance exhausted resources and bled many a pocket dry as they struggled to retain sufficient staff and accommodation, while upholding an impeccable sense of style and luxury. This growing pressure within and outside the government gradually soured the climate.

A fraction of the samurai continued to be employed as servants to the *daimyo*, but the peace brought forth by the Tokugawa era crushed the demand for these warriors. As a result, hundreds of thousands of samurais were turned into roaming *"ronin,"* or "master-less samurai." The life of a samurai was all they knew, and the disillusioned became directionless. Many would forgo their *bushido* code, turning to a lifestyle of looting, pillaging, and deviance as they roved aimlessly throughout Japan.

In conjunction with these developments, historians believe that the unofficial origins of the Yakuza go back to as early as 1612. During this time, officials began to hone in on the growing order of ostentatious rogues known as the *"kabukimono."* The *kabukimono* were often viewed as a nuisance of a society, having been around since the preceding Sengoku era, a tumultuous time punctuated with political conflict, violent upheavals, and general unrest. The *kabukimono*, which translates to either "eccentrics," or "the crazy ones," were unbranded, but they were far from pleasant. They were also known as the *"hatamoto-yakko,"* or "servants of the shogun," and were made up of a band of over 500,000 *ronin*. These *ronin* consisted of both the young and old, as well as samurai sons who would never inherit a more powerful title in their families, and rebellious aristocrats.

The *kabukimono* were agitators, rabble-rousers, and challengers of norms. They were regularly seen loitering around town in garish and gaudy kimonos, with some rocking women's or European clothing. Instead of conventional topknots, their hair and beards grew free and untamed, whereas some featured chrome domes and other unorthodox haircuts. They swaggered around town, showing off the large and lethal swords tucked into their red sheaths. These hoodlums were also known for their loud and obnoxious conversations in nearly indecipherable slang. They were violent and impulsive, often inciting brawls, rowdy singing, dancing, and impromptu booze fests on the streets. While the *kabukimono* did not abide by the *bushido*, they were staunchly faithful to their own kind.

A contemporary depiction of a member of the *kabukimono*

Though the history of the *kabukimono* might ring a bell, the modern Yakuza claim their ancestors had come from a much more humble class of warriors: the *machi-yakko*. These were assemblages of villagers that united to fight back and defend peasants, shopkeepers, and merchants from *kabukimono* or *ronin* raids. Though they were nowhere near as trained or lavishly armed as the samurai, the *machi-yakko* possessed the same courage, earning them choruses of praise from venerating villagers.

Even so, while the *machi-yakko* were hailed as heroes, they did not fit into the mold of society.

They would become one of the first to embrace their low status, and they would spark the tradition of tattooing as a rite of masculinity and virility. The *machi-yakko* essentially operated like any other legitimate organization or crime family, providing jobs and stability in exchange for respect and unswerving allegiance. Indeed, they were so intriguing to outsiders that they soon became subject to numerous books and plays.

The first official generation of the Yakuza was born in the mid-18th century. By then, the *machi-yakko* had dissipated into folklore, while those who were left began to dabble in grayer waters. The remnants turned into classical misfits of society, and were classified into 2 groups – the "*bakuto*," or traveling gamblers, and the "*tekiya*," sketchy street salesmen who pawned off black market goods for a living.

The *bakuto* were money-chancers who first introduced the custom of gambling into Japanese society. Despite the profession's negative connotations, the *bakuto* were commissioned by the government to gamble with construction, irrigation, and other manual laborers. They were stationed all over newly constructed highways, enticing passersby with dice and card games. In doing so, the government hoped to win back some – or if they were lucky, all – of the funds they had shelled out for these projects.

Not only were the *bakuto* the first to undergo the arduous and painful process of full-back tattoos, they were also responsible for giving the Yakuza their name. In the ancient Japanese card game *hanafuda*, or "flower cards," each player received a trio of cards. Like the game of Blackjack, the sum of a player's card determined their score. The worst hand was "20," which could be achieved by the unlucky set of "8-9-3" – to break it down, "**ya**ssu-**ku**-**san**." Critics nicknamed them the "*yakuza*," slang for "loser," effectively dubbing them the slimy bottom feeders of society.

The *tekiya* were not unlike the snake oil swindlers and pretentious potion peddlers of the West. They had also emerged under the Tokugawa reign, forming a network of black market vendors with an awful reputation for selling third-rate or defunct merchandise. Items were often sold by vendors who feigned inebriation, which made potential customers believe that they were swiping up a heck of a deal, only to return home aggravated, and sorely disappointed. They, too, operated on a hierarchy, a common pattern in Japanese and many modern societies. Strangely enough, the *tekiya* were not illegal, and were even allowed to carry 2 swords at a time, allowing for easy intimidation and violence.

While the public had nothing good to say about the *bakuto* or *tekiya*, they mostly skated by with little to no problems. Though they were unscrupulous, they were efficient and kept to themselves, rarely wandering out of their territories. Before long, however, that would change.

The Way of the Yakuza

"If you are not able to kill a human being, you are not qualified to be a Yakuza. If you are not ready to take your own life, you are also not qualified to be a Yakuza." – Daikaku Chodin, a former member of the Yakuza

As with every other business, the Yakuza was run by a board of directors that met frequently to discuss goals and improvements with the operation. The earliest meetings were held in private bath houses. This was ideal, both because they could display their tattoos and because weapons could not be concealed.

Between 1735 and 1749, gang wars had erupted between rivaling groups of *tekiya*. Worse yet, fraud had grown rampant within the community. To rectify this, the government created the *oyabun*, or in English, "foster parents." *Oyabun* were placed at the top of the hierarchy, which headed the *tekiya*. They were now allowed to adopt surnames for their families, and they could legally be armed with swords and weapons, a right previously only granted to the samurai.

The Yakuza also began to start families of their own. The *oyabun*, or *kumicho*, wore the pants in the family. His protégés were known as *"kobun."* The father-son relationship was sacred within the Yakuza; as their name suggests, the *oyabun* were surrogate parents, and often encouraged the *kobun* to leave their past lives behind. The Yakuza was their family now.

As the big boss man, the *oyabun* was naturally the most revered and feared above all within the Yakuza. The *oyabun*'s word was law. The next level comprised of a trio of senior officials, the *saiko-komon* and the *so-honbuncho*, otherwise known as the "Administration," and the *wakagashira,* or the "First Lieutenant." The *so-honbuncho* was the second-in-command as the chief of headquarters, whereas the *saiko-komon* was the *oyabun*'s most trusted sidekick, serving as a senior adviser on the board. The *wakagashira* was the regional manager, and was tasked with managing and supervising the families in their territories.

Under the *wakagashira* were the *fuko-honbucho,* managers who answered directly to their *wakagashira* superiors. The *shateigashira*, or the Second Lieutenant, was in charge of policing smaller sects alongside the *fuko-honbucho.*

The final tier of the pyramid houses 6 rankings. There was the *shateigashira-hosa,* who were assistants to the *shateigashira,* as well as superiors to the low-ranking members. The *shingiin* were law advisers hired to deal with legal affairs and ensure that they stayed within the boundaries of the law. Then, there was the *kaikei,* who were the family accountants.

The last tier made up the bulk of the family. These were the *kyodai,* or "older brothers," and the *shatei*, their "younger brothers." Finally, there was the *wakashu,* who was either a fresh pledge, or a junior assistant. The *shatei* and *wakashu* spent years attempting to scale the ranks, as these were members who were shown the least respect. Some of the modern Yakuza have taken on more Westernized titles, including "President," "Supreme Councilor," "Chairman of the Executive Community," "Head of Liaison," and many others.

An ex-Yakuza member once said that he, like many others, had been lured in by all the glamour and excitement the Yakuza seemed to ooze, only to be severely disappointed when he was made an errand boy. He was expected to cater to all his *kyodai* and superior's needs, including bussing tables and refilling tea and sake cups during mahjong games.

Like the samurais and the *bushido*, the Yakuza lived by a code of ethics known called the "*Jingi*." The *Jingi* was largely based on the *bushido*, and was designed to reawaken the importance of honor and *ninkyodo*, meaning "the chivalrous way." The Yakuza wanted to set themselves apart from the average delinquent gang. They aimed to always act with honor and defend the defenseless, a goal they hoped would soften their image in the public eye. The general public, or non-Yakuza, otherwise known as "*katagi*," were innocents, and were not to be harmed. Even the *oyabun* himself was not immune from these laws; a violation could mean permanent expulsion from the most coveted seat in the family.

The 4 rules in the *Jingi* were said to have been upheld by the Yakuza for centuries. The first rule expressly forbade members of all rankings from partaking or selling harmful narcotics and any other illegal substances. The consumption of drugs, the Yakuza believed, would rob one of their "personal and communal justice," as the potentially lethal substances not only shortened a man's life but also blurred his morals.

The second and third rule prohibited the despicable acts of theft and robbery. Stealing in itself was disgraceful. While stealing from the community might be viewed by some as a victim-less crime, there were no gray areas in the code. Stealing from the less privileged was doubly worse, as it was a violation of a man's personal justice, which was also defined as an individual's means of sustenance. This is supposedly backed by a motto frequently echoed within the Yakuza – "to help the weak and fight the strong!"

The last code encompassed all indecent acts that clashed with the *ninkyodo*. The Yakuza valued themselves as chivalrous vigilantes who dished out their personal brand of justice and wanted nothing to do with the vermin of society. Acts of unnecessary violence, rape, and murder against the helpless would not be tolerated. A more recent addition to the *Jingi* forbids members from engaging in "unnecessary contact" with the *oyabun* or other higher ups.

Punishments were the most severe when these acts were committed against another family member, associate, or any figure the Yakuza held in high regard. The penalty was vicious but simple – "a life for a life." As an unnamed Yakuza boss put it, "When the Yakuza rob people, deal drugs, when they attack civilians, their family members, or their children – they're no longer Yakuza, just mafia."

Legend has it that the earliest Yakuza chose to fight with their bare hands, and only occasionally used their weapons. It is said that their ancestors had been well-trained in numerous forms of martial arts, relying on their hand-to-hand combat skills to waste their opponents. Only when absolutely necessary did a Yakuza unsheathe his weapon, which was usually a katana. Conversely, the modern Yakuza are known to pack heat, including guns, rifles, and other imported military weapons. That said, it must be remembered that much of the origins and accounts mentioned are told through the Yakuza perspective. Several historians write off these noble beginnings as hogwash, while some say these stories have some truth to them but are greatly exaggerated.

A family within the Yakuza was identifiable through their own crests, known as "*daimon.*" Some families have simpler crests, such as the Yamaguchi-gumi, associated with a diamond emblem with thick borders and a single pillar in its center. Another came in the form of the Toa-kai family crest, a circular emblem with a minimalistic road leading to a horizon, stamped with the "East" character. Other *daimon* were decorated with more complex designs, featuring other Japanese characters, floral patterns, or elements of nature. Senior officials carried around gilded *daimon* badges. *Daimon* can also be found printed upon the business cards of the modern Yakuza.

Alexander Krivács Schrøder's picture of the Yamaguchi-gumi crest

Eric Talmadge, the author of *Getting Wet: Adventures in the Japanese Bath*, wrote, "[Yakuza] would...wear pins with the logos of their gangs right there on their lapels for anyone to see, congregate in headquarters with big signs out front saying exactly which gang they were with...One of my sources...used to send me New Year's cards with the syndicate's logo embossed in gold in one corner."

The *shatei* stuck out in a crowd like a scarecrow in a field of dandelions. They were often younger, fashionable, and cocky, with a habit of flaunting their tattoos whenever the opportunity presented itself. Senior officials were especially difficult to detect, particularly in the modern age, as they were well-groomed and can blend in easily in a sea of *katagi*. Some *shatei* spent their entire careers not knowing the identity of some higher-ranking officials, as they were so far apart in the hierarchy that they barely crossed paths, if ever.

The Yakuza also developed their own slang within their families. Some called their *oyabun* "*oyaji*," a street term for "father." Younger *shatei* referred to their glinting katanas and other swords as "*dosu*." To alert their brothers of incoming policemen or authority figures, they cried out, "*satsu*," or "*pori*." Contact with police must have been more than frequent, as an alternative term for search and arrest warrants was coined "*fuda*."

Violations of codes, disrespecting superiors, failure to complete tasks, and treachery against the family were unforgivable sins. The most heinous crimes committed by Yakuza members earned them a death sentence, or they were at least brutally battered to the brink of it. The most popular and chilling form of punishment was a self-mutilating apology called "*yubitsume*." A brother who has done wrong dropped to their knees and laid out a pristine white cloth in front of him, observed by his stoic brothers, who formed a ring around him. Without shedding a tear or producing the faintest of sounds, as expected in Yakuza culture, the blank-faced brother raised his knife over his head and sliced off his little finger, above the upper knuckle. In a few cases, a member with a lower ranking would be tasked with doing the deed, which showcased the guilty brother's remorse and humility. The *yubitsume* was also a member's only way out of the family. Those who wanted a fresh start often presented their severed fingers to their superiors, but even then, not all were released. After all, it is as they say – once a Yakuza, always a Yakuza.

Why the little finger? It is said that this custom was borrowed from either samurai or *bakuto* culture. The pinkie strengthened one's grip on a sword, and this punishment made the guilty weaker. He was forced to rely on the *oyabun* and his family, thereby cementing his once faulty loyalty. *Bakuto* were also known to settle gambling debts with their fingers. Despite their apparent protection and love for the public, the *katagi* did their best to avoid men with stubs for pinkies.

Perhaps one of the most intriguing aspects of Yakuza culture are their striking, often incredible tattoos. There was no special uniform issued to the Yakuza, but a shared aesthetic that has united them throughout the ages was the art on their bodies. Yakuza tattoos are usually full sleeve ink work that either stop short by one's wrists and ankles or are mapped out across their entire body. This includes even the most sensitive points on one's body, including under the arms and on their rib cages. Those with full-body tattoos usually left a clean strip down the middle of their front torsos so they could still wear their kimonos open.

Unlike their ancestors, most of the Yakuza, especially the older members, tend to hide their tattoos. Their body art was not designed to intimidate the public but was meant to be shown only to their Yakuza family. It was a test of how much pain one was able to endure.

This special tattooing method is known as the art of *tebori,* which literally translates to "carved by hand." It is an excruciating process that takes years, sometimes even decades, to complete. Since much of the ink is toxic (and was even more toxic back in the day), members could only be tattooed 2-3 hours per session. These special inks are concocted through a process known as "*sumi.*" Wooden blocks, or "cakes," are used to ground and mix pigment upon a *suzori,* or a smooth stone bed moistened with water. As for the actual tattooing instrument, a finely pointed steel spike is tethered to a long bamboo rod with silk or metal clips. These spikes come in many sizes and are first sharpened against a sandpaper file before being used.

Red, green, yellow, and indigo were the most common colors used in traditional *tebori.* Red ink continues to be the most poisonous of all, stirred up from a blend of iron sulfate and green vitriol, extremely dangerous substances. Those with red ink on their bodies are seen as the toughest in all the family, as only small patches of red could be inked on at a time before the poison would trigger fevers, hives, or debilitating fatigue. A large stamp of the tattoo artist's name can also be found somewhere within his work, their names enlarging in size as their popularity and reputation grows. Yakuza consider the artist's signature another bragging right, as this indicates their wealth and status.

In spite of the grueling pain and its known dangers, the Yakuza continue to use the *tebori.* Tattoo artists usually sit down and interview their client about their lives before their tattoos are created, as it would be designed to tell the client's personal story. Most choose to be inked with mythical or historical Japanese figures. One example is Fudō Myōō, or the "Immovable," a dark guardian of Buddhist treasures, and a fierce spirit that destructs anything its path. Samurai tattoos are generic but meaningful, as they remind the brother to abide by the *jingi* and *bushido.*

A medieval depiction of Fudō Myōō

Symbolic animals and nature are also common requests. The koi fish is perhaps the most common among the Yakuza. Not only did koi represent good fortune, they swam against the current, and were rebels of the water. Apart from dragons, tigers, and other alpha creatures, flowers, such as cherry blossoms and chrysanthemums, were also popular choices. In the documentary *Marked: Death of the Yakuza*, an ex-con and former member explained why he had chosen chrysanthemums, which were typically used for Japanese funerals. According to the ex-con, if he were to die in the middle of nowhere, with no one to visit his grave, he would be able to rest easy, as he would already have himself covered.

Stan Shebs' picture of koi fish

In Japanese culture, special gatherings and celebrations for successful business deals revolved around the *sakakuzi*, which were traditional sake ceremonies. To the Yakuza, the *sakakuzi* served a different purpose, as they were used for initiations. There were 4 types of *sakakuzi* – the *atomesouzoku* (the succession, or passing of the torch); *oyakosakazuki* (parent-child); *kyodaisakazuki* (brother-brother); and *nakanaorisakazuki* (reconciliation). Initiations were formal and spectacular events. An altar was set up in a purified room that had been cleansed of negative spirits and energy. 3 scrolls were placed upon the altar, which paid tributes to a threesome of deities, their names depending on the family. The 12 candles arranged around the altar would be lit, which represented the 12 animal zodiacs of Japan. Other offerings on the table included a sake bottle and cup, 3 dollops of salt, and a pair of raw seabream fish, one bigger than the other as a symbol of the coming parent-child relationship. Later in the ceremony, a filled cup of sake was placed in front of the *oyabun*. The *oyabun* tipped back half the sake and would pass the rest to the initiate, who drains the cup. The cup was then wrapped in decorative paper and placed in the initiate's pocket, which solidified his eternal loyalty to the *oyabun*.

Though they remain a subject barely analyzed by historians, the Yakuza women have been vital. Yakuza wives were called "*gokutsama*," and they mostly played passive roles within the syndicate. They adhere to the *jingi*, but they do not participate in Yakuza activities. These women are often scorned by society, since the Yakuza, despite their apparent noble intentions, are still seen as thugs.

While it is said that some high-ranking officials of the Yakuza had been female, and maybe a boss or two of smaller families, this is not certain. What did exist were the *onna-oyabun*, or "female godmothers." The *onna-oyabun* were especially active after World War II, running black organizations and shady businesses of their own in Tokyo and Yokohama. That aside, most historians agree that they no longer exist today.

Year of the Yakuza

"If new warships are considered necessary we must, at any cost; build them; if the organization of the army is inadequate, we must start rectifying it from now; if needed be, our entire military system must be changed." – Baron Hayashi Gonsuke

Around the mid-19th century, the authority of the Tokugawa shoguns began to lose steam. While the shogunate promoted peace and prosperity among its people, the circumspect government began to grow leery of foreign powers, issuing several bans and restrictions that upset the public. In the height of Japanese Catholicism in 1610, there were roughly 300,000 Christians in Japan. A disorganized and violent suppression of Christian protests in the Shimabara Peninsula from 1637-1638 had forced all the Bible-believers into hiding. Meanwhile, an increase in drought, famine, and natural disasters, as well as a decline in agricultural techniques, only escalated the shogunate's undoing. With that, the shogunate's reputation quickly decayed.

Opposing parties swooped in to take advantage of the new opportunity, aiming to drive the shogunate into extinction and reclaim imperial power. These 2 forces, collectively known as the "Satchō Alliance," were the anti-Tokugawa feudal domains of Satsuma and Choshu. They collaborated to bring 14-year-old Emperor Mutsuhito Meiji, known by his admirers as "Meiji the

Great," back to the throne. This 1868 movement to uproot the foundations of the Tokugawa regime was known as the "Meiji Restoration." "Meiji," named after the emperor, translates into "enlightened rule."

Meiji

The Japanese espoused a more receptive and innovative attitude towards the future, thrusting the nation into the modern age, and severing all ties with feudalism. In this period of enlightenment, the Japanese reopened their doors to foreign trade but kept the influence of Western ideology to a minimum, and they continued the mission to extinguish Christianity.

The restoration, which lasted until the death of the emperor in 1912, also brought a number of reforms. One of its most important reforms was on education. The Japanese knew that modernization could only be achieved through proper education and training, so a new system called the "*gakusei*," was established in 1872, which completely reshuffled and improved the system and curriculum. There were more schools and universities, as well as specialty institutions and technical learning centers, which helped satisfy the growing demands of new labor and technology. Primary school also became obligatory for both boys and girls. Though attendance started out low, by 1906 it was at 95%, and the soon boasted one of the highest literacy rates in the world.

By the end of the Meiji era, Japan had become a centralized bureaucratic government with an elected parliament. Not only were they now more educated, they hosted a brand-new transportation system, as well as spiffy financial and government structures. Most importantly, it boasted the most powerful military Japan had ever seen.

As the Meiji Restoration marked the end of the nation's isolation to the outside world, trade thrived. A new wave of small and medium-sized businesses cropped up all over the country. Unfortunately for professional gamblers, mainly the *bakuto*, their careers were effectively over, as gambling was made almost entirely illegal. The only forms of gambling that were allowed, such as horse or boat racing, were now heavily supervised, and had to abide by new sets of unbendable guidelines.

This new crackdown on crime rocked Japan's criminal underworld. The Yakuza knew their only chance at survival was to discover new options of making money, even if it meant going against the precious *jingi*. As the surviving Yakuza began hunting for new opportunities, what was left of the *bakuto* and *tekiya* joined forces to form their own Yakuza families. Some of these new families chose to single out lawmakers, and they were often hired by dishonest politicians who would use the hired muscle for bribery, blackmail, votes, and even the occasional murder of a political rival.

In most cases, the origin of the Yakuza family determined the type of business they were in. The *bakuto* now ran underground gambling joints, hiring its own to act as bankers and bodyguards. Other *bakuto* Yakuza built chains of *nomiya* to pay the bills, which were private gambling houses devoted to horse racing. Others were loan sharks that collected debts through blackmail and intimidation. Families of *tekiya* controlled marketplaces, and managed the street stalls in almost all festivals throughout the year. If merchants coughed up a small fee, the Yakuza would protect them from competitors, and ensure the visibility of their stalls. These protection rackets would become so popular within the Yakuza that it continues to be one of their most common sources of income.

Yakuza who were descended from *gurentai*, or in English, "city thugs," were perhaps the wildest and most unpredictable of all families. These were the true rebels of society with no tangible backgrounds, and they felt no obligations to any codes of ethics. These troublemakers were said to have been happy to do anything – and they meant, anything – if it meant getting their hands on cold, hard cash.

The last group of the new breed of families came from the *uyoku*, the Japanese version of political right wing extremists, as well as traditionalists, nationalists, anti-communists, and more. They were characterized by their hatred for mammoth corporations, which they believed were manipulating the economy. *Uyoku* Yakuza often harassed corporation officials through blackmail, intimidation, and nasty shake-downs. A few *uyoku* claim that a fraction of the profits taken were distributed back to the small fries in the business world, but again, there is little to no evidence.

Other Yakuza families during the Meiji period were big-time pimps who ran prostitution rings and badger games. Badger games were crafty extortion schemes involving a beautiful young woman, usually a prostitute, seducing an unsuspecting man. The man was invited back to her home, where a jealous husband, a role played by a Yakuza, would abruptly emerge, wielding a cleaver or some other weapon. If the victim was married, the "husband" threatened to pay his wife a visit. The browbeaten men would have no choice but to comply, leaving the house unsatisfied and their pockets turned inside out.

As time progressed, more of the Yakuza began to drift farther and farther away from their codes of honor. New black market businesses came with the modernization of technology and society, from the less serious piracy of music, movies, and other media, to the atrocious trafficking of women and children. It is said the Yakuza control not only the red light districts but also the lucrative businesses of pornography, strip clubs, and erotic brothels.

Some have more than violated the first rule of the *jingi*. *Philopon*, or "ice," a type of crushed, crystal-like methamphetamine, was one of the most frequently moved products within the Yakuza drug circles. The drug became especially popular during World War II, and it was advertised as the perfect way to keep awake and keep one's crippling hunger at bay. Factory workers snorted ice to work longer hours, while soldiers kicked back and inhaled them to stay more vigilant during battle. Some kamikaze pilots are said to have consumed the product before their missions. Today, it is said that the Yakuza make several million U.S. dollars on ice every year.

The modern Yakuza are also accused of operating reputable construction and real estate firms behind the scenes. They are also owners of pachinko parlors (arcade games similar to slot machines), tourism centers, and even talent agencies. The most astute Yakuza officials are even said to be involved in the Japanese stock market. *Sokaiya* are stock-owning thugs who storm into and terrorize the meetings of corporation executives, extracting bribes with supposed company secrets as leverage.

One of the most sensationalized *sokaiya* scandals revolved around Mitsubishi in the 1990s, and it saw a string of its firms implicated in the misconduct. In 1997, a pair of Yakuza *sokaiyas* were arrested, and Terubo Tei, one of the conspirators, admitted to police that they had spied on Mitsubishi for months, learning of the allegedly dishonest business tactics discussed during boardroom meetings. In an effort to keep them silent, the corporation decided to pay up. Between 1995 and 1997, over 9 million yen ($80,550 USD) was transferred into the *sokaiya* accounts. 20 other companies were also accused at the same time, and both Toshiba and Hitachi were also found to have been tipping the *sokaiya* 500,000 yen ($4,475 USD) in cash on a yearly basis since 1986.

The Yakuza have continued to explore a slew of unethical but interesting professions. An *atariya* was a professional car crash dummy. These con artists hurled themselves in front of vehicles, then demanded compensation. A *jisageya,* or "real estate price wreckers," were hired to move in to affluent communities and act as rowdy as can be, their presence causing the market value to plummet. Once these devalued lands were purchased by their *oyabun*, the *jisageya* promptly packed up and left. The market value would once again, soar, and the land was then resold for double or triple the initial investment. Fake clubs and organizations were also set up by the Yakuza to solicit donations from the public, which went straight to their pockets.

Some of the most magnificent buildings in the city served as Yakuza headquarters, with the family's name and crests displayed for all passersby to see, almost taunting them. The Yakuza even ran their own newspaper, the *Yamaguchi-gumi.* Even in the mid-20th century, there were no laws against money laundering, which only accelerated the Yakuza's growth. Dr. Joseph Siracusa, a Yakuza expert and lecturer, noted, "It's like a generation of the mob in the United States had gone legitimate...the money is now out there in the corporate world, and there is nothing you can do about it."

After a lull during World War II, the Yakuza comeback was in full swing, and by the 1960s, there were an estimated 184,000 members. To put this in perspective, this number was equivalent to half of the entire Japanese police force in 2010. There were more foreign initiates than ever, and these foreign newcomers were known as the *sangokujin*, meaning "people from 3 countries" – Korea, China, and Taiwan.

Once again, like any other business, the Yakuza soon decided it was time to expand their operations. By the 1980s, the Yakuza had established bases as far as Western Europe, South America, and the Gold Coast of Australia. They were on a roll, and it did not look as if they would be stopping any time soon.

The Japanese began to migrate to Brazil in the 1930s to seek refuge from the war, taking up menial jobs as manual or agricultural laborers. After the war, an even larger tide of Japanese immigrants arrived in Brazil, hoping for a new life. Though Brazil already had its hands full with their fair share of crimes and societal dilemmas, the Yakuza created their own niche market in the Liberdade District of Sao Paulo. The Yakuza in Brazil were known for extortion scams, drug trafficking, prostitution rings, and illegal immigrant mills.

In time, the Yakuza and various European criminals and syndicates bonded over a shared interest in gun smuggling. One of the earliest known cases was in 1965, when a pilot from Air France was arrested for smuggling firearms to the Yakuza. In 1982, a Yakuza was stopped and searched by the side of the road, after which he was discovered to be harboring 300 Garesi handguns and 20,000 Milanese bullets. The extra security forced the Yakuza to wade around their pools of creativity; for example, in 1995, police confiscated 1,300 miniature guns imported from Austria.

The Yakuza would become active in the United States, too, predominantly in Hawaii but also in Nevada, California, and New York. Hawaii was perhaps the most ideal location for underground street racing competitions, as well as the smuggling of goods, due to its location. The Yakuza in California mostly operate in Los Angeles, which has long been a breeding ground for aspiring actresses and models. It is said that these women had been ensnared by the pretense of advancing their career portfolios, only to be shoved into a world of pornography and the sex trade.

Icons and Adversaries

"Fewer people want to become Yakuza. But those who do will be very logical, very scary and much, much more dangerous." – Manubu Miyazaki, son of a Yakuza member

Over time, more and more young men became drawn to the glitz and glamor associated with the Yakuza. Much like the allure of the Italian Mafia or Triad Gangs, lost and often troubled souls latched onto these families, envisioning greatness, fancy gadgets, women, and power. These eager beavers often overlooked the discipline and perseverance required to become a Yakuza. Manubu Miyazaki remarked, "They think being a Yakuza is like joining a company. There's a joke about a young man going to a gang office and asking what the salary was, and would he get insurance."

These misguided youngsters were in for a rude awakening. It is said that there are 2 types of Yakuza – clan and freelance. A clan-minded Yakuza is one that is well-informed about the reality of what the job entails, whereas the freelancers were nothing more than inked, overambitious pretenders and small-time street hustlers. A clan-minded Yakuza is by far the rarer of these breeds.

Making a name for oneself in a swarm of contenders competing for the same prize is a strenuous and winding journey. While many give up before they reach their destination, it is not unachievable. In every lane of crime, there is a figure that succeeds in pawing their way to the top. There was Pablo Escobar, the storied kingpin of the Medellín Cartel, an operation that once raked in over $60 million USD daily in cocaine and drug money. There was Al Capone, the fedora-toting mobster powerhouse who exploited the black market during the Prohibition Era. And then, there were the big shots of the Yakuza.

Japan entered its industrial age in the early 20th century, after the Meiji Restoration. While the economic boom that followed did wonders for the nation, the skies dimmed over the Yakuza. Authorities continued to zero in on devious businesses, shutting down surviving gambling arenas run by *bakuto* gangs. Even though the *tekiya* had long been stigmatized for their crooked stalls and questionable product, they remained technically legal, and continued to coast by.

The *uyoku* Yakuza prospered, as they had followed the footsteps of their ancestors during the Meiji era. To prevent harassment and crackdowns, they teamed up with greasy authorities and carried out favors and under-the-table deals for them. It would not be long before democratic reforms were introduced to Japan, which spawned vocal opponents in the forms of communist, socialist, and militarist parties. Militarists bred their own secret armies trained in warfare, blackmail, and other aggression tactics. They struck a deal with the *uyoku*, who gladly supplied training, equipment, and manpower.

The Yakuza had certainly seen better days, but the younger generations only seemed to become more fearless – overweening, even. A trend of smart black suits, white dress shirts, oversized sunglasses, and short, crisp haircuts caught on with the new generation, paying tribute to the American gangster movies that had been all the rage at the time. Swords were stowed away, and in place, the Yakuza brandished pistols and firearms of all sizes.

Despite the incessant changes of the ever-evolving Yakuza, one unassuming fisherman remained undaunted. This was Harukichi Yamaguchi, a poor laborer from Awaji Island who founded the Yamaguchi-gumi family in 1915. Rather than risk the dangers of tackling an area he knew nothing about, Harukichi utilized the valuable experiences and knowledge he had accumulated from his fisherman days. Following Yakuza tradition, he dove right in to the business of protection rackets.

Knowing that the Yakuza was under scrutiny, Harukichi knew he needed to keep a low profile. He started small, managing the docks at Kobe. Once profit was steady, he began to branch out, selling his services to numerous businesses across the city.

One of the major keys to the Yamaguchi-gumi's success was their chain of shrewd, no-nonsense leaders. The seat of *oyabun* was not given to the man with the most kills under his belt, but wise, business-minded torchbearers who knew how to take their operation to the next level. After a decade, Harakuchi was succeeded by his son, 23-year-old Noburu. Noburu might have been young, but he had been exposed to the crime family for over 10 years, and for the next 5, Noburu strengthened the fledgling company and created a monopoly, gaining almost complete control over Kobe's food market.

As critical as the father and son were, it was the third *oyabun* that would transform the company into the global behemoth that it is today. This was Kazuo Taoka, who was barely 24 months old when the family was created. Like many of the most influential names in history,

Taoka had a rough childhood; he was orphaned at a young age, received only minimal education before he moved to Kobe, earning a measly paycheck as an apprentice at a shipbuilding yard. Taoka's name was far from foreign in the community, and in fact, was almost always the talk of the town. The scrappy young man, nicknamed "Taoka the Cutter," was a trained boxer and fighter with a volatile temper, who once beat up his own boss at work.

Mitsuru Ono, Kazuo Taoka, and Kōji Tsuruta in 1952

Taoka began to fraternize with local thugs, and his petty thefts escalated into aggravated assault and murder. He would do his time for each charge. A few years later, Noburu was fatally wounded in a turf war and died in October 1942 at the age of 41. The sudden death left the Yamaguchi-gumi with no successor. By then, Taoka had a wife and family, and he had mostly cleaned up his act, but as he turned 33, he was invited to become the third *oyabun* of the leaderless family.

When Taoka took his seat on the throne, the Yamaguchi-gumi had a moderate membership of 30 men. As Taoka ventured into extortion, gambling, loan sharking, smuggling, and more black market businesses, the membership went through the roof. At the time of Taoka's death 35 years later, the Yamaguchi-gumi had become the largest criminal syndicate in Japan, a status that still stands today. Not only do they run a Yakuza newspaper and magazine, they had even launched their own website in 2014, entitled the "Banish Drugs and Purify the Nation League." The website featured the family's own theme song, and it included an anti-drug message in the hopes of purifying their tainted image. That year, there were reportedly 23,400 members in the family, approximately 44% of the entire Yakuza population. According to Forbes, the family alone hauled in an unbelievable $6.6 billion USD that year, and about a total of $80 billion in its lifetime.

Another key figure in Yakuza history is Yoshio Kodama. While Kodama was not an *oyabun*, this *uyoku* at heart would one day be known as the "Postwar Yakuza Grandfather." Born in 1911, Kodama spent most of his childhood with his relatives in Korea. To his relatives, it was no secret that Kodama had always shown an avid curiosity in right-wing politics, but never could they have imagined what would become of him. At 21, Kodama, along with other conspirators, were arrested for plotting the assassination of the prime minister and select high-ranking cabinet officials. His foiled plan landed him in prison for 3-and-a-half years.

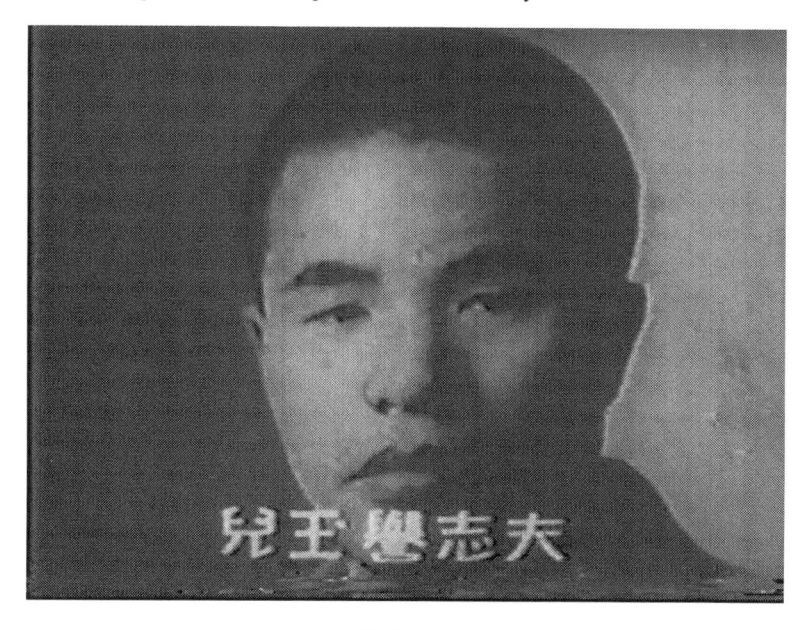

Kodama

Kodama was eventually released, and out came a man with a change of heart. Kodama began to work as a "fixer" for the very men he once tried to get rid of. He maintained a network of spies across Asia, mostly in China, and obtained classified information about the enemy. The intel was then passed back to authorities, and for this, he was paid handsomely. Meanwhile, he helped smuggle shiploads of radium, copper, nickel, and cobalt into Japan to aid his country during World War II. Not one to pass up an opportunity, he also snuck in packages of heroin and other narcotics in the shipments. For his help, Kodama was later awarded the title of Rear Admiral, and by the time Japan surrendered to Allied forces, Kodama had a jaw-dropping net worth of $175 million USD.

Kodama may have been filthy rich, but his nation's surrender came with a price. He was labeled a Class A war criminal by Allied forces and was sentenced to another 2 years in prison. The seemingly imperturbable Kodama kept his head down and served his time with no complaints. When he was released, he picked up where he left off, and his ambitions now knew no boundaries. Not one to hold a grudge, Kodama acted as a middleman for Allied forces and the Yakuza. He provided Yakuza manpower and equipment to complete all tasks assigned by the Allies, and he collected substantial fees for his work. His glowing reputation in the criminal underworld soon took off, and he was praised for his efficiency and people skills. His track record showed his expertise in disrupting communist activities and upholding peace between criminal and political parties, and he was even said to have brokered deals with the CIA.

In the 1960s, Kodama used his peacemaking skills to cease the tensions between warring Yakuza families. He even helped formed an alliance between Taoka of the Yamaguchi-gumi and Hisayuki Machii of the Tōsei-kai, a South Korean gang based in Tokyo. However, his name was sullied when he became embroiled in a scandal in the mid-70s; Kodama was accused of using his position to unfairly squeeze the Lockheed Corporation, an American aerospace company, into the Japanese market, pocketing $2.1 million in the process. Before a verdict could be reached, Kodama suffered a stroke and died in his sleep.

The Yakuza's success did not go unnoticed by rival criminal gangs. Deciding that they also wanted in on the Yakuza-manned black market, competitors fought for some of that action. Kabukicho, Japan's red light district, was (and continues to be) one of the most prominent of all Yakuza strongholds. These neon-kissed streets span about 100 square blocks, and they are lined with restaurants, arcades, karaoke bars, hostess clubs, love motels, and other sleazy establishments. Chinese gangs in Kabukicho were determined to infiltrate that market. They moved in quickly and slashed their prices, undercutting the Yakuza in not just Kabukicho but a variety of criminal services. A Chinese hit man, for example, cost only $2,700 USD, a little more than half of what it cost to hire a Yakuza hit man.

The Chinese gangs only grew bolder. Stories circulated about Chinese gangsters barging into Yakuza establishments, threatening staff and customers with weapons in broad daylight. Another incident in Yokohama illustrates the barbarous determination of the Chinese gangs. Most of the shops there were in cahoots with the Yakuza, which infuriated Chinese gangsters. Tired of the Yakuza's antics, a mob of Chinese gangsters poured into a Chinese restaurant, and one of these gangsters, armed with a cleaver, lopped off the head of a waiter in front of the horrified patrons. Their message was clear – they were the new boys in town.

Not surprisingly, Yakuza competitors are far from a new phenomenon. Another notable case took place shortly after World War II, when Japan's morale was at an all-time low. Over 5.1 million Japanese people returned home, which took a toll on the already depleting resources. Inflation was inevitable, and the black market became one of the only options for the most basic of necessities. While the citizens suffered, the black market blossomed. The curses of this blessing were the turf wars and unrest that ensued between competing gangs. By now, it was common knowledge that the Yakuza was more than protective of their territories, and that they were less than happy about the Formosan gangs breaching their domain. The bubbling racism on both ends did not help matters. Things were bound to get ugly.

In June 1946, an epic rumble erupted between members of Formosan and Matsuba-kai Yakuza gangs, right outside the Shibuya Police station. Over a thousand Yakuza faced off with hundreds of Formosan gangsters, swinging clubs, metal pipes, and pistols. The Shibuya police, who tried to contain the situation, would later be condemned for their incompetence in handling the situation. This unsavory event is now known as the "Shibuya Incident."

Crashing Tides and Public Discontent

"We have existed this long because the police allowed us to exist, and we have cooperated with them to some extent. Those days are gone. We are being replaced internally and externally by thugs and gangs who make no pretense of having any codes at all." – A former Yakuza boss

Contrary to popular belief, the Yakuza were far from invincible. As with business, downturns and phases of hardship and loss were unavoidable. In the 1980s, the Yakuza, along with many other Japanese corporations, enjoyed bountiful profits from the nation's domination over the global market. Little did they know that things that were too good to be true often were.

The occupying Allied forces that settled in Japan after the war made a considerable impact in molding the nation's economical progress. The United States began a sound and durable business relationship with Japan, which helped bring the nation back on its feet. In the years that followed, Japan exported millions of dollars worth of products to the United States.

The *zaibatsu,* or in English, "financial cliques," had been the heart and soul of the Japanese economy during the Meiji period. These were diversified family-controlled monopolies that included Mitsubishi Bank, Mitsubishi Motors, and many more. The *zaibatsu* system ensured concentrated power, as the majority of these leaders were related by blood or marriage. However, the new economy saw the decline of the *zaibatsu.* A new system of conglomerates surfaced, known as the "*keiretsu.*" These companies were a fusion of businesses connected by cross share-holders. The *keiretsu* shrugged off the importance of familial ties, and instead, united with other businesses that matched their banking and company interests. This, *keiretsu* supporters insisted, would promote growth and stability.

While the *keiretsu* had their advocates, they also had detractors who condemned them for unfairly hogging the market. The small and medium-sized businesses were left in the dark, and did not stand a chance against this faulty new system. Nevertheless, the *keiretsu* conglomerates expanded their operations. They started off by duplicating and improving Western products, which they then sold back to the Westerners for a large discount. Japanese manufacturers became the golden geese of the worldwide market, desired for their affordability, and attention to quality and detail. Towards the 1970s to the 1980s, Japan steered its attention towards the electronics market, and soon, prevailed in that field as well.

At this stage, Japan was known as the "King of the Global Electronics Industry." They held a monopoly in almost all the major lanes of the market, including circuit boards and semiconductor chips. At one point, people were convinced that Hitachi and Sony, two of Japan's leading electronics brands, would one day own IBM and other American competitors, toppling the U.S. market.

At this point, Japan was at its prime. Its standard of living, national currency, and even life expectancy rates, were higher than they had ever been. Their GDP rates were almost double the statistics of many Western nations, and the nation had also become the world's largest creditor. But unbeknownst to the public, the Japanese were trapped in a bubble, and it was about to burst.

In 1989, the Nikkei, the stock market index for Japan, took a massive hit, dropping from 39,000 to 20,000 in less than a year. By 1992, it was at 15,000. Companies suffocating with debt disintegrated one after another, while others kept their heads above water only thanks to government bailouts. This dark era was aptly nicknamed the "Lost Decades." The news of the bubble burst spelled trouble for the Yakuza. Members of the public who had once viewed them as semi-heroic figures had completely turned their backs on them. The Yakuza were shunned from neighborhoods, and less and less people wanted anything to do with them. As business for the Yakuza began to spoil, turf wars escalated, further pushing away the frightened and repulsed public.

The government finally stepped in to stuff a cork in the outrage. Starting in 1991, a series of anti-gang laws were issued, mostly aimed at the Yakuza. That year, the Prefectural Public Safety Commissions passed the "Anti-Boryokudan Act." The *boryokudan* was another term for a Yakuza, but it was also applied to gangs "likely to facilitate its members to collectively or habitually commit illegal acts of violence." The first decree announced that all *boryokudan* were now required to officially register with the police. The Yamaguchi-gumi, Inagawa-kai, and Kudo-kai, were some of the first to sign up in 1992. Those named in this list were prohibited from engaging in any of the crimes listed in the act, encompassing involvement in firearms, drug trafficking, and other criminal activities.

It became easier to track and shut down so-called gang offices. Search warrants were granted more frequently, which allowed authorities to sweep through Yakuza and *boryokudan* headquarters. High-ranking officials could now be persecuted for the crimes committed by their lackeys. The National Center for Elimination of *Boryokudan* was later established to investigate *boryokudan* and black market crimes. In the year 2000, the police were also granted use of wiretaps.

On top of the mounting pressures brought about by the probing eyes of the authorities, trouble brewed within the Yakuza. As expected, many of these internal conflicts centered on the syndicate's largest family – the Yamaguchi-gumi. In August 1984, 51-year-old Masahisa Takenaka was elected as the *oyabun*, but his short-lived reign would last just 5 months. One day, upon leaving his mistress' apartment in Osaka, a black car rolled up and wound down its windows, gunning down Takenaka and 2 of his lieutenants. The orchestrator was said to have been part of the Ichiwakai gang, a faction that broke away from the Yamaguchi-gumi when Takenaka took control. Takenaka's funeral was a glorious sight to behold. More than 1,000 gangsters in ink-black suits poured into the streets for the funeral procession. 400 Japanese policemen were dispatched to the scene with riot shields, batons, and other protective gear.

Yet another tragedy that transpired as a result of the power struggle within the Yamaguchi-gumi took place in 1997. The second-in-command, and rumored successor to the *oyabun* seat of the family, Masaru Takumi, would also experience the element of surprise when he was gunned down in a coffee shop. The perpetrators were said to have been from another breakaway faction known as the "Nakano-kai." At least one innocent bystander was also killed after being hit by a stray bullet.

To this day, the internal rivalry still persists, and based on recent reports, the unrest in the Yamaguchi-gumi family is far from over. One of the family's newest opponents comes in the form of yet another renegade faction called the "Kobe Yamaguchi-gumi." Members of both companies have been accused of plowing their cars into competing headquarters and homes of senior officials.

With all these measures and restrictions put in place, along with their burgeoning unpopularity with the public, the Yakuza retreated into the shadows. Most of the Yakuza began to cover up their tattoos, and younger generations were no longer as easily charmed or swayed by the seemingly dying culture of the Yakuza. In the 1990s, a bizarre sort of surgery that produced finger prosthetics began to trend across the nation. Not only did this help the current Yakuza blend in, former members and victims visited clinics. Apart from regaining the strength of their grip, they hoped their finger attachments would improve their chances when it came to job hunting, granting them a new lease on life.

Angels and Demons

"Nothing but Ninkyodo, that is the man's way of life. The way by duty and compassion, bearing the ordeal for our dream." – An excerpt from the Yamaguchi-gumi anthem

Some may be mortified by the idea that there are those who not only tolerate the Yakuza but commend these explosive families. There are some who have ceased their support somewhere along the way as the families continued to deviate from their code of ethics, and there are those who never took kindly to them in the first place. As boggling as it may be to many, some point naysayers to the philanthropic and charitable deeds carried out by the nation's most powerful crime syndicate.

Particularly in recent years, the Yakuza have been of immense help to relief efforts. In most cases, these terrifying families arrived at the devastated scenes hours before the authorities did. One such incident came during the Kobe earthquake in January of 1995. The dreadful earthquake swayed the land back and forth for well over 20 seconds and hit 6.9 on the Richter scale, the worst to have ever struck the region. The calamity claimed the lives of 6,425 people, severely injured 25,000, and rendered another 300,000 homeless. The Yamaguchi-gumi was the first to mobilize, sending thousands of their men to the ruined cities to personally distribute food, water, and other supplies. The Yamaguchi-gumi headquarters were in Kobe, but it suffered minimal damages. The family opened its doors and ushered in wandering and disoriented crowds who had no place to go. Members of the family even helped patrol the streets to prevent looting and riots

The kind efforts of the Yakuza proved to be more than a one-time deal. They would once again come to the rescue during the terrible tsunami and earthquake that ravaged Japan in March of 2011. The dismal disaster wiped out over 22,000 residents. Hundreds of thousands more were made homeless, and 2,500 remain missing to this day. This time, the fast-acting aid was a collaborative effort made by the Yamaguchi-gumi, Inagawa-kai, and Sumiyoshi-kai families. Less than an hour after the first shockwave, all 3 families in Tokyo opened their doors once more to displaced residents. 2-ton trucks, along with whatever vehicle could be scrounged up at the time, arrived, bearing food, blankets, and water. The next day, 25 more 4-ton trucks pulled up to the survivors' camps, packed with ramen, diapers, flashlights, first-aid kits, and other necessities amounting to about $500,000 USD. A senior official of the Sumiyoshi-kai was even said to have reached out and aided the foreign communities that were affected. This step in unification was seen as a great leap for the progressives of Japan, as the nation was known for its uninviting and xenophobic attitudes towards foreigners.

Inevitably, many took note of the Yakuza's self-effacing presence during the relief efforts. Yakuza members were said to have worn thick jackets and scarves and kept their sleeves rolled down so that residents would not be alarmed. Witnesses reported their appreciation and gratitude for the ostensibly trivial but extra mile the Yakuza went to in order to help. One member of the Yamaguchi-gumi allegedly confided to Jake Adelstein, a reporter for *The Daily Beast,* "Please don't say any more than we are doing our best to help. Right now, no one wants to be associated with us, and we'd hate to have our donations rejected out of hand."

In addition to the generosity the Yakuza displayed during those trying times, they were also said to have acted as valuable assets to the authorities on occasion. One such case involved an unlikely partnership formed between the Yakuza and the Japanese police in the 1990s, which was overseen by retired police detective, Akihito Saruta. At this point in time, the Yakuza was feeling the heat of all the fresh laws and decrees issued against the *boryokudan*. This led the Yakuza, albeit grudgingly, to striking a deal with the cops. Under this agreement, the Yakuza would pass along vital information, clues, and evidence to authorities, which helped them solve current investigations involving murder, theft, and other violent crimes, as well as resurrect cold cases. It might have seemed unconscionable, but it was a win-win situation on both ends.

While both parties proved to work quite well together, it was important for them to remember that certain boundaries were never to be crossed. They could be civil – even friendly – with one another, but they were not allowed to, under any circumstances, get too close with one another.

These peculiar partnerships are now a thing of the past; it is now forbidden for the police to work with the Yakuza. This was bittersweet – while this practice was considered immoral to many, it has become much more difficult for authorities to gather sufficient evidence, which has allowed many criminals to get away with crimes.

All of that aside, do a few instances of largesse cancel out all the tragedy and mayhem that the Yakuza has wreaked upon Japan? For one, authorities and Yakuza critics claim that the Yakuza's charity is riddled with ulterior motives. With the positive press, the tongue-tied authorities could say nothing bad about the Yakuza without appearing ungrateful. Better yet for the Yakuza, the positive press made it easy for them to win bids for several reconstruction projects that followed, and they subsequently raked in the "dishonorable" profits.

The Yakuza are often portrayed as cool-as-sin gangsters with hip and flair for days, propagated in part by movies, comics, and other media. The syndicate's modern recruitment tactics prey on this, with some claiming it acts as a kind of grooming for future members. Statistics show that quite a large percentage of Yakuza initiates today are plucked from local middle and high schools, as well as teenage delinquents, often homeless or runaways.

Japanese authorities urge the public to remember the innocent lives lost in the hands of the vengeful Yakuza. Besides the numerous politicians who have been slain by Yakuza hit men, even mere critics, or those who have offended the family in some way, were and continue to be targeted. In August 1990, author Atsushi Mizoguchi, who refused to retract a hostile piece he had written about the Yakuza, had a knife plunged in his back. He would later recover, but the perpetrators were never caught. 2 years later, famous director, Juzo Itami, whose extensive line of work included satire about the Yakuza, would also find himself on the wrong side of the syndicate. The Yakuza was anything but pleased with Itami's newly released film, which depicted the Yakuza as heartless thugs who were humiliatingly defeated by a female lawyer before the credits rolled. One day, as Itami began to unlock his front door, he was ambushed by Yakuza thugs with samurai swords. They slashed up his face and left him to bleed out. Itami required several stitches and a brief stint in the hospital, but thankfully, he, too, survived.

Indeed, it appeared that the smallest slight against the Yakuza could land one in hot water – in 1999, a junior high school principal from Osaka was pummeled and stabbed by a Yakuza gangster for refusing to raise a flag.

Young boys may be easily seduced by the suave, women-filled lifestyles allegedly led by the Yakuza, but one must not ignore the cruel reality behind the Yakuza-controlled sex industry of Japan, an operation that has since spread worldwide. Most hostess clubs and "love" establishments have been described by authorities as a "hotbed of human trafficking." Quite a few of these families have also dipped their toes into child pornography.

On the other hand, perhaps this brush must not be painted over the Yakuza as a whole. A former member, Shinji Isihara, has publicly denounced and expressed regret over the new generation of child-exploiting Yakuza. A disgusted Isihara revealed, "If a Yakuza who are above a certain rank did this kind of business and were arrested, they would be disgraced."

The Modern Yakuza

"The more the police push, the more the Yakuza are simply going underground, making their activities harder to follow than they ever were before." – Shoku Tendo, daughter of a senior Yakuza official

The Japanese government's mission to eliminate the Yakuza for good continues to this day. In 2006, new initiatives were set in place to ban the Yakuza and other suspected *boryokudan* from taking part in the stock market, as well as sport-related businesses and other fields of public entertainment. These initiatives encouraged companies and businesses that had fallen victim to the Yakuza to step forward. On an even brighter note, companies affiliated with the Yakuza were blacklisted, and all funding was instantly ceased.

Over the next 2 years, more decrees were passed to prohibit the extortion and intimidation of government officials, regardless of political party. These crimes were classified as an "act of violent demand," and the guilty were now found responsible for "economic damages," earning them harsher prison sentences. Furthermore, this new law prevented gangsters from pressuring officials into handing over business contracts.

Another mandate entitled "The Law for the Punishment of Organized Crimes and Control of Crime Proceeds and Other Matters" declared that all funds and valuable property collected from prostitution, gambling, and other illegal houses would be placed in a government-owned fund as "crime-related profits." In October 2007, stricter measures were also tacked on to gun laws, with 30 million yen ($265,470 USD) as a maximum fine, as well as a sentence of 5 years to life for gun violence committed in the name of any *boryokudan*. New laws in 2011 were also issued to penalize companies for ties to any criminal organization.

Despite these laws, the Yakuza have always been a chameleon in the face of adversity, and they have continued to hold their own. In the early 2000s, Yakuza were said to have still controlled more than 5,500 street stalls, 3,000 lending agencies, and 2,000 spas, strip clubs, restaurants, and construction firms each. Not only have they adapted to the ever-changing environment, they are also said to rank on top in the prison hierarchy. Some say even the guards do what they can to avoid them.

To keep up with modern times, the Yakuza have penetrated the world of electronic commerce. To minimize Yakuza profits, credit card companies are now prohibited from conducting business with adult entertainment establishments, but as always, the Yakuza have found a loophole. Adult stores partnered with the Yakuza continue to advertise that they accept credit cards, in hopes of fooling customers into thinking that they are legal, government-approved entities. Charges from these bills are handled by a third-party credit facility. Instead of the usual 3% processing fee, the customer is charged 15%, and the Yakuza receives a 10% cut.

Today, the Yakuza footholds around the world still enjoy steady growth. While its current membership does not hold a candle to the Yakuza's heyday, they are still over 70,000 members strong. More so, their legacy as one of the largest operating crime organizations in existence continues, with the Yamaguchi-gumi family in the lead. As terrifying as the truth may be, the Yakuza are here to stay, and they are far from bidding their last farewell – at least, not anytime soon.

Online Resources

Other books about the Yakuza on Amazon

Bibliography

1. Johnson, Adam. "Yakuza: Past and Present." Organized Crime Registry. Tripod, Inc., Feb. 2007. Web. 6 Feb. 2017. <http://orgcrime.tripod.com/yakuzahistory.htm>.

2. Editors, Iromegane.Com. "History of Yakuza." IROMEGANE.COM. IROMEGANE.COM, 12 June 2015. Web. 6 Feb. 2017. <http://www.iromegane.com/japan/culture/history-of-yakuza/>.

3. Jones, Terril Yue. "Yakuza among first with relief supplies in Japan." Reuters. Reuters Group plc, 25 Mar. 2011. Web. 6 Feb. 2017. <http://www.reuters.com/article/us-yakuza-idUSTRE72O6TF20110325>.

4. Editors, Japan Subculture. "Yakuza Organisations." Japan Subculture. Japan Subculture Research Center, 11 Jan. 2013. Web. 6 Feb. 2017. <http://www.japansubculture.com/resources/yakuza-organisations/>.

5. Nakajima, Stephanie. "Women of the Yakuza." Japan Subculture. Japan Subculture Research Center, 18 Feb. 2014. Web. 6 Feb. 2017. <http://www.japansubculture.com/wives-of-the-yakuza/>.

6. Adelstein, Jake. "The Yakuza Code Of Ethics: Compliance In the Underworld." Japan Subculture. Japan Subculture Research Center, 15 Oct. 2011. Web. 6 Feb. 2017. <http://www.japansubculture.com/the-yakuza-code-of-ethics-compliance-in-the-underworld/>.

7. Joy, Alicia. "A Guide To Traditional Japanese Art Forms." The Culture Trip. The Culture Trip, Ltd., 23 Sept. 2016. Web. 6 Feb. 2017. <https://theculturetrip.com/asia/japan/articles/a-guide-to-traditional-japanese-art-forms/>.

8. Maria. "Eat Like A Japanese – 11 Dishes You Must Try." Nerd Nomads. Nerd Nomads, Ltd., 26 May 2016. Web. 6 Feb. 2017. <https://nerdnomads.com/japanese-food>.

9. Schott, Joe. "The Weirdest Japanese Game Shows: Bottomless Pits, Boobs & Mummification." Heavy. Heavy, Inc., 13 Sept. 2012. Web. 6 Feb. 2017. <http://heavy.com/comedy/2012/09/the-weirdest-japanese-game-shows-bottomless-pits-boobs-mummification/>.

10. Hongo, Jun. "Nearly 20 Million Tourists Visited Japan Last Year." The Wall Street Journal. Dow Jones & Company, Inc., 19 Jan. 2016. Web. 6 Feb. 2017. <http://blogs.wsj.com/japanrealtime/2016/01/19/nearly-20-million-tourists-visited-japan-last-year/>.

11. Editors, JRef. "Sengoku Period." Japan Reference. Xenforo, Ltd., 10 Apr. 2013. Web. 6 Feb. 2017. <https://www.jref.com/articles/sengoku-period.232/>.

12. Editors, New World Encyclopedia. "Edo period." New World Encylopedia. MediaWiki, 12 Sept. 2013. Web. 6 Feb. 2017. <http://www.newworldencyclopedia.org/entry/Edo_period>.

13. Editors, Japan Guide. "Samurai." Japan Guide. Japan Guide, Ltd., 11 Apr. 2014. Web. 6 Feb. 2017. <http://www.japan-guide.com/e/e2127.html>.

14. Editors, History Channel. History Channel. A&E Television Networks, LLC, 2015. Web. 6 Feb. 2017. <http://www.history.com/topics/samurai-and-bushido>.

15. McKay, Brett, and Kate McKay. "The Bushido Code: The Eight Virtues of the Samurai." The Art of Manliness. The Art of Manliness, Inc., 14 Sept. 2008. Web. 6 Feb. 2017. <http://www.artofmanliness.com/2008/09/14/the-bushido-code-the-eight-virtues-of-the-samurai/>.

16. Editors, My Learning. "Japanese Samurai Armour." My Learning. My Learning, Ltd.,

2012. Web. 6 Feb. 2017. <http://www.mylearning.org/japanese-samurai-armour/p-4304/>.

17. Kurihara, Juju. "History of Japanese Tattoo." IROMEGANE.COM. IROMEGANE.COM, 16 Apr. 2013. Web. 6 Feb. 2017. <http://www.iromegane.com/japan/culture/history-of-japanese-tattoo/>.

18. Ashcraft, Brian. "Japan's Problem with Tattoos." Kotaku. Gizmodo Media Group, 29 Mar. 2016. Web. 6 Feb. 2017. <http://kotaku.com/japans-problem-with-tattoos-1767685623>.

19. Adelstein, Jake. "Types of yakuza and their businesses." Japan Subculture. Japan Subculture Research Center, 6 May 2012. Web. 6 Feb. 2017. <http://www.japansubculture.com/types-of-yakuza-and-their-businesses/>.

20. Editors, Nakasendoway. "Sankin Kotai and the Hostage System." Nakasendoway. Walk Japan, Ltd., 2016. Web. 6 Feb. 2017. <https://www.nakasendoway.com/sankin-kotai-and-the-hostage-system/>.

21. Szczepanski, Kallie. "The Yakuza of Japan." About Education. About, Inc., 6 Feb. 2017. Web. 6 Feb. 2017. <http://asianhistory.about.com/od/japan/fl/The-Yakuza.htm>.

22. Grabianowski, Ed. "How the Yakuza Works." How Stuff Works. InfoSpace Holdings, LLC, 2015. Web. 6 Feb. 2017. <http://people.howstuffworks.com/yakuza1.htm>.

23. Editors, Japan Subculture. "Yakuza Group Structure." Japan Subculture. Japan Subculture Research Center, 24 Nov. 2011. Web. 6 Feb. 2017. <http://www.japansubculture.com/resources/yakuza-group-structure/>.

24. Editors, Highsnobiety. "A Beginner's Guide to the Yakuza." Highsnobiety. Titel Media GMBH, 29 Oct. 2015. Web. 6 Feb. 2017. <http://www.highsnobiety.com/2015/10/28/yakuza-beginner-guide/>.

25. Raz, Jacob. "Insider Outsider: The Way of the Yakuza." Kyoto Journal. Heian-Kyo Media, 7 Aug. 2014. Web. 6 Feb. 2017. <http://www.kyotojournal.org/the-journal/society/insider-outsider/>.

26. Kovacs, Imre. "What are the names of the different ranks within the Japanese yakuza?" Quora. Quora, Inc., 29 May 2015. Web. 6 Feb. 2017. <https://www.quora.com/What-are-the-names-of-the-different-ranks-within-the-Japanese-yakuza>.

27. McNeill, Daniel. "New-look yakuza tries to become the friendly face of Japan." The Independent. Associated Newspapers, Ltd., 2014. Web. 7 Feb. 2017. <http://www.independent.co.uk/news/world/asia/new-look-yakuza-tries-to-become-the-friendly-face-of-japan-9233641.html>.

28. Adelstein, Jake. "Goodbye to the Yakuza." The Atlantic. The Atlantic Monthly Group, 1 Oct. 2011. Web. 7 Feb. 2017. <https://www.theatlantic.com/international/archive/2011/10/goodbye-yakuza/337236/>.

29. Dougherty, Caroline. "YAKUZA." Outsider Japan. PB Works, 2010. Web. 7 Feb. 2017. <http://outsiderjapan.pbworks.com/w/page/9758567/Yakuza>.

30. Buren, Peter Van. "Why Do The Yakuza Cut Off The Tips Of Their Little Fingers?" Xpat Nation. Xpat Nation, Ltd., 16 Sept. 2015. Web. 7 Feb. 2017. <http://xpatnation.com/why-do-the-yakuza-cut-off-the-tips-of-their-little-fingers/>.

31. Myers, Christopher. "16 Beautiful Yakuza Tattoos and Their Symbolic Meaning." Ranker. Ranker, Inc., 2015. Web. 7 Feb. 2017. <http://www.ranker.com/list/yakuza-tattoo-meanings/christopher-myers>.

32. Editors, TYPT. "Sakazuki." The Yakuza: Pinkyless and Tattooed. WordPress, 14 Dec. 2015. Web. 7 Feb. 2017. <https://yakuzahistory.wordpress.com/sakazuki/>.

33. Editors, CHIN. "Education During the Meiji Restoration, Japan." Canadian Heritage Information Network. CHIN-Canadian Heritage Information Network, Ltd., 1999. Web. 7 Feb. 2017. <http://www.virtualmuseum.ca/edu/ViewLoitLo.do?method=preview&lang=EN&id=12991>.

34. Editors, AFE. " The Meiji Restoration and Modernization." Asia for Educators. Asia for Educators, Columbia University, 2010. Web. 7 Feb. 2017. <http://afe.easia.columbia.edu/special/japan_1750_meiji.htm>.

35. Koh, Michael. "15 Scary Things You Didn't Know About The Yakuza." Thought Catalog. The Thought & Expression Company, LLC, 2014. Web. 8 Feb. 2017. <http://thoughtcatalog.com/michael-koh/2014/02/15-scary-things-you-didnt-know-about-the-yakuza/>.

36. Willacy, Mark. "Old-style Yakuza regret child pornography push." ABC News. ABC AU, 20 Oct. 2009. Web. 8 Feb. 2017. <http://www.abc.net.au/am/content/2009/s2718553.htm>.

37. Editors, Tofugu. "JAPAN, LAND OF THE RISING METH." Tofugu. Tofugu, LLC, 10 Apr. 2012. Web. 8 Feb. 2017. <https://www.tofugu.com/japan/meth-in-japan/>.

38. Johnston, Eric. "From rackets to real estate, yakuza multifaceted." The Japan Times. The Japan Times, Ltd., 14 Feb. 2007. Web. 8 Feb. 2017. <http://www.japantimes.co.jp/news/2007/02/14/reference/from-rackets-to-real-estate-yakuza-multifaceted/#.WJ1movl95PZ>.

39. Editors, Japan Times. "More Mitsubishi firms tied to 'sokaiya' payoffs." The Japan Times. The Japan Times, Ltd., 24 Oct. 1997. Web. 8 Feb. 2017. <http://www.japantimes.co.jp/news/1997/10/24/national/more-mitsubishi-firms-tied-to-sokaiya-payoffs/#.WJ1mqfl95PZ>.

40. Editors, Japan Times. "Mitsubishi Motor funds were payoffs: 'sokaiya'." The Japan Times. The Japan Times, Ltd., 10 Nov. 1997. Web. 8 Feb. 2017. <http://www.japantimes.co.jp/news/1997/11/10/national/mitsubishi-motor-funds-were-payoffs-sokaiya/#.WJ1msPl95PZ>.

41. Jenkins, Philip. "DESTROYING JAPANESE CHRISTIANITY." Patheos. Patheos, Inc., 7 Feb. 2014. Web. 8 Feb. 2017. <http://www.patheos.com/blogs/anxiousbench/2014/02/destroying-japanese-christianity/>.

42. Sutton, Susan. "Japan's Long and Bumpy Road to a Legalized Casino Industry." Casino News Daily. Casino News Daily, Inc., 31 July 2015. Web. 8 Feb. 2017. <http://www.casinonewsdaily.com/2015/07/31/japans-long-and-bumpy-road-to-a-legalized-casino-industry/>.

43. Lies, Elaine. "Gangster daughter sheds light on Japan underworld." Reuters. Reuters Group plc, 3 Sept. 2007. Web. 8 Feb. 2017. <http://www.reuters.com/article/us-japan-gangsters-idUST26750520070903>.

44. Editors, Hub Pages. "Top 5 Mafia Bosses Of The Last 100 Years." Hub Pages. HubPages, Inc., 21 July 2014. Web. 8 Feb. 2017. <http://hubpages.com/entertainment/Top-5-Mafia-Bosses-of-the-Last-100-Years/>.

45. Hays, Jeffrey. "YAKUZA AND ORGANIZED CRIME IN JAPAN: HISTORY, HONOR, PUNCH PERMS, PINKIES AND TATTOOS." Facts and Details. N.p., Apr. 2012. Web. 8 Feb. 2017. <http://factsanddetails.com/japan/cat22/sub147/item811.html>.

46. Schreiber, Mark. "Mags go big for Kobe gang's 100th." The Japan Times. The Japan Times, Ltd., 17 Jan. 2015. Web. 8 Feb. 2017. <http://www.japantimes.co.jp/news/2015/01/17/national/media-national/mags-go-big-kobe-gangs-100th/#.WJ1m3fl95PZ>.

47. McCurry, Justin. "Japanese gang war feared as largest yakuza syndicate splits." The Guardian. Guardian News and Media, Ltd., 7 Sept. 2015. Web. 8 Feb. 2017. <https://www.theguardian.com/world/2015/sep/07/japan-yamaguchi-gumi-yakuza-split-fear-gang-war>.

48. Editors, TYPT. "Yamaguchi-gumi." The Yakuza: Pinkyless and Tattooed. WordPress, 15 Dec. 2015. Web. 8 Feb. 2017. <https://yakuzahistory.wordpress.com/yamaguchi-gumi/>.

49. France-Presse, Agence. "Japanese mobsters launch their own website." The Guardian. Guardian News and Media, Ltd., 2 Apr. 2014. Web. 8 Feb. 2017. <https://www.theguardian.com/world/2014/apr/02/japanese-mobsters-launch-website-yakuza>.

50. Hays, Jeffrey. "MAJOR YAKUZA GROUPS AND LEADERS: YAMAGUCHI-GUMI, YOSHIO KODAMA, KENICHI SHINODA,TADAMASA GOTO." Facts and Details. Jeffrey Hays, Jan. 2013. Web. 8 Feb. 2017. <http://factsanddetails.com/japan/cat22/sub147/item2303.html#chapter-7>.

51. Spacey, John. "Kabukicho: Tokyo's Infamous Entertainment District (50 Photos)." Japan Talk. Japan Talk, Ltd., 2 Sept. 2009. Web. 8 Feb. 2017. <http://www.japan-talk.com/jt/new/kabukicho-tokyos-infamous-entertainment-district>.

52. Staff, Tokyo Reporter. "Yakuza feud continues with more car-ramming incidents." The Tokyo Reporter. The Tokyo Reporter, Ltd., 3 Mar. 2016. Web. 9 Feb. 2017. <http://www.tokyoreporter.com/2016/03/03/yakuza-feud-continues-with-more-car-ramming-incidents/>.

53. Colombo, Jesse. "Japan's Bubble Economy of the 1980s." The Bubble Bubble. WordPress, 4 June 2012. Web. 9 Feb. 2017. <http://www.thebubblebubble.com/japan-bubble/>.

54. Editors, ENotes.com. "Explain the difference between the zaibatsu and keiretsu. ." ENotes.com. ENotes.com, Inc., 27 June 2012. Web. 9 Feb. 2017. <https://www.enotes.com/homework-help/explain-difference-between-zaibatsu-keiretsu-346207>.

55. Hays, Jeffrey. "LAWS AIMED AT FIGHTING THE YAKUZA." Facts and Details. Jeffrey Hays, Jan. 2013. Web. 9 Feb. 2017. <http://factsanddetails.com/japan/cat22/sub147/item1786.html>.

56. Editors, NPA. "2. Fight against Organized Crime." National Police Agency . National Police Agency Japan, 2016. Web. 9 Feb. 2017. <https://www.npa.go.jp/english/kokusai/pdf/POLICE_OF_JAPAN_2016_16.pdf>.

57. Haberman, Clyde. "TV FUNERAL FOR JAPAN'S SLAIN GODFATHER." The New York Times. The New York Times Company, 1 Feb. 1985. Web. 9 Feb. 2017. <http://www.nytimes.com/1985/02/01/world/tv-funeral-for-japan-s-slain-godfather.html>.

58. Talmadge, Eric. "JAPANESE POLICE MOBILIZE TO AVERT GANG WAR AFTER MURDER OF MOB BOSS." AP News Archive. The Associated Press, 5 Sept. 1997. Web. 9 Feb. 2017. <http://www.apnewsarchive.com/1997/Japanese-police-mobilize-to-avert-gang-war-after-murder-of-mob-boss/id-08553266a1c468b32d20b75eb0994860>.

59. Jozuka, Emiko. "The Woman Who Makes Prosthetic Pinkies for Ex-Yakuza Members." Motherboard. Vice Media, 9 Feb. 2016. Web. 9 Feb. 2017. <https://motherboard.vice.com/en_us/article/the-woman-who-makes-prosthetic-pinkies-for-ex-yakuza-members>.

60. Adelstein, Jake. "Yakuza to the Rescue." The Daily Beast. The Daily Beast Company, LLC, 18 Mar. 2011. Web. 9 Feb. 2017. <http://www.thedailybeast.com/articles/2011/03/18/japanese-yakuza-aid-earthquake-relief-efforts.html>.

61. Harrison, Kristi. "5 Inspiring Acts of Kindness by Terrifying Crime Syndicates." Cracked. Cracked Entertainment, Inc., 16 Dec. 2009. Web. 9 Feb. 2017. <http://www.cracked.com/article/238_5-inspiring-acts-kindness-by-terrifying-crime-syndicates/>.

62. Hays, Jeffrey. "KOBE EARTHQUAKE OF 1995." Facts and Details. Jeffrey Hays, July 2011. Web. 9 Feb. 2017. <http://factsanddetails.com/japan/cat26/sub160/item863.html>.

63. Editors, CNN . "2011 Japan Earthquake - Tsunami Fast Facts." CNN. Turner Broadcasting System, Inc., 22 Nov. 2016. Web. 9 Feb. 2017. <http://edition.cnn.com/2013/07/17/world/asia/japan-earthquake---tsunami-fast-facts/>.

64. Efron, Sonni. " Japanese Director Juzo Itami Recovering After Gangland-Style Stabbing at Home : Crime: Attack may have resulted from his latest film, which debunks mobsters. He calls on public to fight back." Los Angeles Times. Los Angeles Times, Inc., 26 May 1992. Web. 9 Feb. 2017. <http://articles.latimes.com/1992-05-26/news/mn-155_1_juzo-itami>.

65. Adelstein, Jake. "Host clubs: a hotbed of human trafficking." The Japan Times. The Japan Times, Ltd., 5 Apr. 2014. Web. 9 Feb. 2017. <http://www.japantimes.co.jp/news/2014/04/05/national/host-clubs-a-hotbed-of-human-trafficking/#.WJ1uG_l95PZ>.

66. Ollman, Bertell. "Why Does the Emperor Need the Yakuza? Prolegomenon to a Marxist Theory of the Japanese State." Dialectical Marxism. Bertell Ollman, 2004. Web. 9 Feb. 2017. <https://www.nyu.edu/projects/ollman/docs/yakuza.php>.

67. Adelstein, Jake, and Nathalie Kyoko Stucky. "Where Have Japan's Yakuza Gone?" The Daily Beast. The Daily Beast Company, LLC, 9 Mar. 2014. Web. 9 Feb. 2017. <http://www.thedailybeast.com/articles/2014/03/09/where-have-japan-s-yakuza-gone.html>.

68. Matthews, Chris. "Fortune 5: The biggest organized crime groups in the world." Fortune. Time, Inc., 14 Sept. 2014. Web. 9 Feb. 2017. <http://fortune.com/2014/09/14/biggest-organized-crime-groups-in-the-world/>.

69. Kaplan, David E., and Alec Dubro. Yakuza: Japan's Criminal Underworld. California: U of California Press, 2012. Print.

70. Treverton, Gregory F., Carl Matthies, Karla J. Cunningham, Jeremiah Goulka, Greg Ridgeway, and Anny Wong. Film Piracy, Organized Crime, and Terrorism . N.p.: RAND Corporation, 2009. Print.

71. Nicaso, Antonio, and Marcel Danesi. Made Men: Mafia Culture and the Power of Symbols, Rituals, and Myth. N.p.: Rowman & Littlefield Publishers, 2013. Print.

72. Ikegami, Eiko. Bonds of Civility: Aesthetic Networks and the Political Origins of Japanese Culture (Structural Analysis in the Social Sciences) . Cambridge: Cambridge U Press, 2005. Print.

73. Chou, Chan Tan. "Battling the Yakuza." 101 Yakuza. Al Jazeera English. 16 Aug. 2012. Television.

74. Boag, Philip. "Death of the Yakuza." Marked. National Geographic. 15 Oct. 2009. Television.

Free Books by Charles River Editors

We have brand new titles available for free most days of the week. To see which of our titles are currently free, click on this link.

Discounted Books by Charles River Editors

We have titles at a discount price of just 99 cents everyday. To see which of our titles are currently 99 cents, click on this link.

Printed in Great Britain
by Amazon